Preface

The author, Thomas R. Wims, is passionate about his advocacy for civil rights. Growing up in Tuskegee, Alabama, on Logan Street, during the civil rights era, he experienced racial injustice at an early age, which greatly influenced him. He also learned how to address racism and discrimination in a constructive manner. He was taught by the best, family members, neighbors, and community members.

While he witnessed unjust behavior much too often, he is committed to identifying patterns of injustices and taking corrective action before the worst situation occurs. In 2025, he sees a return to the violent tendencies and mindset of the civil rights era, the 1950s and 1960s.

Why is the USA repeating the same mistakes 60 years later? How did the people of the US forget the trauma of the civil rights era and re-impose unjust laws and tolerate the unjust application of laws in a discriminatory manner? The US is harassing immigrants, imposing tariffs, and attacking our allies.

His goal in writing "Who Are You in 2026? A Moral Dilemma," is to start a conversation with each reader where the reader is encouraged to do some self-reflection. This book informs, inspires, and educates the reader. However, the big question is, "What are you, the reader, going to do to save the United States?"

ISBN # 979-8-9949664-1-9

Table of Contents

© Copyright

1 Introduction

We are living in a time of moral dilemmas in the US. We see unethical and unjust actions daily on the news, that gas lights each and every person. We see the promotion of division, not unity in the United States. The question to each of you is," What are you going to do about it?" 2025 and early 2026 have been a period of chaos in the US. Attacks on immigrants, tariffs on our international trading partners, threats on our allies, termination or restrictions on visa, for over 100 countries, elimination of Diversity Equity and inclusion (DEI) programs in the federal government, and the massive reduction in force of inspectors general and the Department of Justice are just a few of the things that have traumatized all people in the US and around the world. Chaos has reigned supreme.

This book provides an overview to our years of chaos and asks the most defining question of our collective lives. Questions of the year. – Who are you in 2026? What are you going to do to fix the US?

Are you living your life <u>Morally Right</u> or <u>Morally Wrong</u>? Think about this for a minute? We know our parents taught us right from wrong to the best of their ability, which was peppered with their implicit biases. Once you understand the current make up of our country versus 1950, you may find the definition of morally right and wrong has shifted. Based on who raised you and where you grew up, the definition of morally right and wrong varies. If you were taught that people of certain religions, or skin color or country of origin were beneath you, (we will call them "those people",) then you have been trained to have an implicit bias in determining right from wrong. For instance, if you family members described those people as being less capable than you in athletics, science, languages and general intelligence, you believed it.

There is also the application of laws and customs to be considered. Prior to the 1950's some show owners declined to serve people of color, even though their signs indicated they were open for business to serve all. Was it morally right or wrong to withhold service from a group of customers? When law enforcement officers' ticket "those people" many times more often that your people, this is seen as selective enforcement of laws. Is this practice morally right or wrong? Where do you stand on the issue of morality in everyday life?

Now, let's dive into it. First let's define Morally right and wrong.

"Morally right" (as defined by the Cambridge Dictionary) refers to actions, decisions, or beliefs that align with established ethical principles, social norms, or conscience regarding good and proper behavior. It implies actions that are just, virtuous, and beneficial, often contrasted with actions that cause harm or break ethical codes.

Key Aspects of Being Morally Right:

- Ethical Alignment: Actions conform to accepted moral codes, principles, or rules.
- Virtuous Behavior: Behaviors that are honest, kind, and just.
- Conscience-Driven: Guided by an inner sense of duty, fairness, and ethical judgment.
- Contextual Differences: What is considered morally right can be determined by societal norms, or, according to some perspectives, by universal standards or, in some cases, the majority view

- Intent and Result: It involves both having good intentions and producing outcomes that are considered good or proper.

Components and Examples:

- Virtue: Acting with honor and high moral principles.
- Duty: Fulfilling obligations or doing the "right thing".
- Fairness: Treating others with respect and in a socially acceptable way.

Morally right actions often relate to, but are distinct from, legal rights, focusing more on moral, rather than legal, justification.

Examples of morally right behavior include, serving all customers in a store. The more customers a business has, usually trends to greater sales and profit. For law enforcement officers, ticketing all people equally, and issuing warnings, equally, are examples of morally right behavior.

"Morally wrong" is the opposite concept. Common synonyms for "morally wrong" include immoral, unethical, sinful, wicked, corrupt, vile, evil, unjust, reprehensible, and unprincipled, all describing actions or behaviors that violate accepted standards of right and wrong.

Strong Synonyms

- Immoral: Deliberately violating moral principles.

- Unethical: Going against professional or societal standards of conduct.

- Sinful: Violating religious or moral laws.

- Wicked: Evil or morally bad in principle or practice.

- Corrupt: Dishonest or depraved, often involving abuse of power.

- Vile/Vicious: Extremely unpleasant, evil, or depraved.

- Evil: Profoundly immoral and wicked.

Other Related Synonyms

- Unjust: Not fair or equitable.

- Reprehensible: Deserving condemnation or censure.

- Unprincipled: Lacking moral principles or guidance.

- Depraved/Degenerate: Morally corrupt; perverted.

- Dishonorable/Shameful: Bringing disgrace or loss of honor.

- Iniquitous: Unjust, wicked, or sinful.

Examples of morally wrong behavior include the shooting of unarmed, immigration protestors in Minneapolis MN in January 2026. Shooting and killing protesters is considered wrong by most people. It is also considered "murder" as defined by the laws in the United States. However, the actions of senior law enforcement to try to spin stories, about the shooting is considered morally wrong by the general population.

When dealing with people on a daily basis, do you act in a morally right or wrong manner? Only you can answer this question. Maybe a better question is, "How do you want the world to treat you, … morally right or wrong?"

At the end of each chapter, you will find a short pop quiz. Please take each one and discuss your answers with friends and family. The discussion with friends may be the most enlightening aspect of this book. You may learn who you really are.

When you take the quiz below, please answer how you feel in most situations. Although you may not feel your answer is 100% right or 100%, please indicate your majority feelings.

Pop Quiz – Introduction – Morally Right or wrong?

#	Question	Right	Wrong
1	Are the 2025- 2026 immigration roundups morally right or wrong?		
2	Was the elimination of DEI programs morally right or wrong?		
3	Was threatening our international allies morally right or wrong?		
4	Was placing seemingly random tariffs on international trading partners morally right or wrong?		
5	Were mass firing of government employees morally right or wrong?		

2   Chaos Years

The years 2025 and 2026 presented massive changes to the lives and livelihoods of people in the United States of America and the world. The objective of this book is to encourage each reader to ask the question "Who am I in 2025 and beyond?" The second objective is to encourage each of you to understand that we the people of the United States need each other. The US population is very diverse with people from all over the world. At the end of each chapter, a short test is available, which will help you reflect on who you are. I encourage you, the reader, to read each chapter and take the short test. Reflect on your answers. I hope this will help you determine "Who You really are."

Consider the following actions of the United States of America in recent months.

- ➤ Immigration reforms and forceful enforcement have resulted in the expulsion of thousands of people from the US. Families have been separated from each other. US citizens have been arrested and detained indefinitely. US citizens have been killed during

Immigration raids. The US government misrepresents the truth about most incidents. The fact is that the people and corporations in the US need to understand that our immigrant population is growing, while the domestic birth rate has dropped below the replacement rate. New immigrants to the US equal new customers, increased tax base, and stronger communities. By blocking immigration, we, the United States, are hurting our own future.

➢ Affordability promises by US leadership have not materialized. Lower prices on day one of the new administration was promised for all. The "What" (lower prices) and "When" (on day one) were stated. But the "How this will be achieved?" and the "How Much big will the price reductions be?" were never answered. Public outcry throughout 2025 has indicated that most people in the US have an affordability problem. If our elected officials, don't hear or believe us, then they are working against the citizens of the US.

➢ Reducing the size of the government. The Department of Government

Efficiency (DOGE) closed several government agencies and ordered the layoff tens of thousands of federal government employees. These actions resulted in significant reductions of government capabilities. Chaos and confusion were introduced in to the operations of the government. The administration stated a goal of increasing employment and making this country financially stronger. However, the administration took actions that are opposite to the stated goals.

➢ America First approach to the world. The US is acting like the Bully and Colonizer of the world. The US demeaned and insulted every NATO, European, African, and Pacific Allies. The actions of the current administration seem to be diminishing or destroying the post World War II allies that have proven to be a successful unit for more than 80 years. Is this administration building peace or destroying peace?

Additional actions implemented by the US against our international neighbors include the following. How can these actions possibly help our country?

- ➤ Destructive tariffs on international trading partners.

- ➤ Insulting our two best trading partners, Mexico and Canada.

- ➤ Threatening to make Canada our 51st state.

- ➤ Threatening to acquire Greenland by force.

- ➤ Loss or denial of "Due Process of Law."

> ## "Who benefits from the chaos in the US?"

A big question for many was, "Who benefits from the chaos in the US?"

- ➤ US citizens – No

- ➤ Immigrants to the US and their relatives - No.

- ➤ Foreign Allies - No.

- ➤ Foreign adversaries. – Yes

- ➤ Domestic terrorist groups, domestic and international criminal organizations - Yes

Is this the United State you want to live in?
Is our government a Dictatorship or
Democracy? Is our government working for
the benefit of US citizens and international
relations? Before we can decide, who we are
as a country, each of us must decide who we
are as an individual. Please read this book,
answer the questions, and discuss your
answers with friends and family.

Pop Quiz – Chaos Years

#	Question	Yes	No
1	Have you and your family benefited from new Trade tariffs?		
2	Have farmers, ranchers, and agribusinesses benefited from trade tariffs?		
3	Is life more affordable in 2025 – 2026 than previous years?		
4	Has the current US government improved relations with foreign allies?		
5	Do you want to treat all immigrants as criminals?		

3   The Pledge of Allegiance

Why do you say the pledge of Allegiance? When do you say it? And most important, what do YOU mean when you make the pledge? Are you pledging to support our "one nation" or just your state and local area? Do you pledge to provide national support to local areas when experiencing disasters? Or, do you support supporting your local are only? By answering these questions, I hope you will be able to better assess, "Who you are in 2025." Let's explore these questions.

Most Americans have learned the Pledge of Allegiance in grade school. In years gone by, it was said in the, morning at school, at the beginning of club meetings, and before athletic events. Most of us say it from memory. I realize that many schools do not recite the "Pledge of Allegiance" on a daily basis any more, however, it is a fundamental part of being a US citizen. Consider this? When was the last time you gave thought to the meaning of our United States "Pledge of Allegiance?"

The U.S. Flag Code provides guidelines for showing respect during the pledge. Civilians should face the flag, place their right hand over their heart, and remove hats. Uniformed military personnel and veterans should stand at attention, face the flag, and render a military salute.

The Pledge of Allegiance is a patriotic oath of loyalty to the United States and its flag. Composed in 1892, it is now part of the U.S. Flag Code. The current version, finalized in 1954, states:

"I pledge allegiance to the Flag of the United States of America, and to the Republic for which it stands, one Nation under God, indivisible, with liberty and justice for all".

Let' s review what we are saying.

a) ***"I pledge allegiance to the Flag of the United States of America, and to the Republic for which it stands,*** - Currently the Republic includes 50 states, the District of Columbia, and six inhabited and administered territories: American

Samoa, Guam, the Northern Mariana Islands (CNMI), Puerto Rico, the United States Virgin Islands, and Wake Island, in addition to numerous uninhabited territories. All of this is considered "The United States of America

b) ***one Nation under God, indivisible, -*** Our nation is supposed to be indivisible. Other than athletic events, we the people pledge to work together and support each other. We pledge to work together for the benefit of all, which automatically includes each one of us.

c) ***with liberty and justice for all".*** – This phrase means, we the people should aspire to guarantee and execute liberty, and justice for all people in this country. "All the people" includes all human beings who are currently in this country, regardless of the citizenship, race, creed, country of national origin, sexual orientation, or religion.

" Most Americans can NOT list the name of all 50 states, and territories with our referring to and Atlas, dictionary or 21 USC § 387(22). (21 U.S. Code § 387 – Definitions)

Do you ever think about what you mean when you say the Pledge? If the pledge includes the United States of America, then it includes the people of each of the states, the District of Columbia, and all territories.

This country is made up of immigrants and decedents of immigrants from around the world. As a matter of fact, you fit into this category.

Consider that historically the people in each state or region, looked and acted in a fairly homogeneous manner. Farmers understand the land, crop cycles, weather effects on the land, and the economics of being a farmer. If you live in a cattle ranch area and culture, you understand cattle and the impacts of nature on cattle ranching, and the economics of cattle ranching. However, if you live in a city, you understand "city life" and the impacts of weather, traffic, and more. The population of the United States includes all of us.

In order to understand the United States, "we the people" should learn to understand the people of the United States. "We the People" includes all residents in this country. According to the US Census Bureau, the following data describes the population of the United States in 2024.

Please note that the population of Whites is declining and the population of minorities is increasing. If you have any doubt of this analysis, read the constitution of the United States, including its 27 amendments. Collectively they are commonly referred to as the "Constitution".

Please take the following Pop Quiz. When you finish, review your answers, and consider what the answers say about you.

> Are you living up to the intent of the "Pledge of Allegiance"?
> Are you a good American to all other Americans?

Think about it. If you don't like your answers about your views, are you willing to change your viewpoint?

Pop Quiz - The Pledge of Allegiance

#	Question	Yes	No
1	Do you say the "Pledge of Allegiance?		
2	Do you agree that the Pledge includes all 50 states and territories and applies to all people living in those areas?		
3	Do you believe that all people in this country are entitled to fair and equal treatment under the law, regardless of age, race, citizenship, religion, sexual orientation, etc., as stated in the Pledge of Allegiance?		
4	Do you believe each person in this country is entitled to being treated with dignity and respect, including you, your family members, and new immigrants?		
5	Do you believe that people of all ethnic and religious backgrounds should serve in the military, law enforcement, first responders, and as elected officials?		

4 The Browning of America. - Who lives in the United States in 2026.

The goal of this chapter is to open our eyes to the fact that the population that we grew up in is NOT the population demographics now. We the people must adjust our thinking to the reality of our current and future trending population. The beautiful diversity of the Unites States is all around you. Open your eyes and see it. People with diverse backgrounds perform essential positions in transportation, medicine, law enforcement, public safety, and virtually every aspect of our lives. We need to appreciate each other. People from virtually every country in the world have immigrated to the United States. Each person has contributed elements of their culture and knowledge that improve our society.

Politicians should recognize that the voter populations of 2028 will not look like the voter population of 2024. The new minority base will be deciding elections and setting priorities for governance. The future is here!

Corporate leaders need to embrace the growing minority population in this country, because they will be your new customers, employees, and stockholders. The future is here!

We the citizens and leaders of the United States, need to understand the reality of the population of this country. Our population is growing along with the world's population. Many of our laws and customs, which were developed prior to 1950 were developed by the people living in that time.

When people say they want to "Make America Great Again.", they are usually referring to the 1950's. What was 1950 like and who lived here. I don't believe we can ever go back to the 1950s.

 In 1950, the US was 89.5 % white, 10% Black / African American, and 0.5% other races. According to the Census bureau, most Hispanics and non-African Americans (aka Blacks, Negro, Colored) were counted as "white". In my opinion, most Hispanic, Latino Americans, Asian Americans, and new immigrants were under counted. Our laws and the administration of our laws were skewed to benefit the 89.5% of the population. Minorities were usually mistreated and undervalued. 2026 Looks very different from 1950. According to the US Census Bureau, our population has grown from about 151,325,798 in 1950 to about 342,312,425 in January 2026. As our population has grown 226.2% since 1950, so should our understanding of our current population.

Minorities are becoming the largest segment of our population. The following data presents who the US has become. In 2026, we have citizens and new immigrants from virtually every country in the world. We are on the tipping point of being a mixed-race country with no majority race. Consider people in this country have married "the one they love" regardless of race, religion, or country of national origin. Therefore, our native-born citizens are claiming a racial status of "mixed or other". That is who we are now. Bye the way, DNA tests are proving that must of us are ancestry in two or more races, and continents of ancestral origin.

A shift in population demographics means a shift in power!

Did you know that our population is trending to be more diverse? The following statistics and projections are from the US Census Bureau and the US Congressional Budget Office.

This population shift has and will continue to change live in the US. As our population grow, so does our employment base. This is vital to a country that will build and maintain vital infrastructure, such as public works, water and sanitation, energy, housing, public health care and safety, roads and defense More working citizens leads to a larger tax base, which pays for our infrastructure. Now let's look back in time. The "Make America Great Again" campaign looked heavily to the nostalgia of the 1950s. Were those years really so great?

Key 1950 Population Demographic Details:

- **Total Population:** 151,325,798.
- **Gender:** Females outnumbered males by roughly 1.43 million, particularly in older age groups.
- **Racial Composition:** 89.5% White, 10% Black, and 0.5% other races.
- **Household Structure:** 87% of households were married; 52% of households included children under 18.

As of January 2026, the United States population is approximately **342.3 million to 349 million**. Demographic trends in 2026 show a significant slowdown in population growth, primarily driven by a historic decline in net international migration and continuing low fertility rates. (Congressional Budget Office Jan 2026 and the US Census Bureau)

Current Population Stats (2026)

- **Total Population:** Estimated at **349,035,494** by mid-year 2026. The U.S. Census Bureau's real-time population clock recorded **342,312,425** as of January 27, 2026.
- **Median Age:** 38.7 years.
- **Urbanization:** 83.1% of the population lives in urban areas.
- **Population Density:** 38 people per square kilometer (99 per square mile).

As you can see the demographics of this country have changed dramatically in the past 75 years. We will never look like 1950 again. We should embrace the evolution of the US.

US Census Bureau Data from 1950 - 2026

Figures based on 1950–2020 Decennial Census data and 2024-2026 projections. Data from 1950 primarily classified by White/Nonwhite, later years include broader, more precise categories.

Census Year	Total Population	% White	% Black	% Hispanic	% Asian/ Other	Tot % (Margin ogf error ,2%)
1950	151.3 M	~89%	~10%	~2-3%*	<1%	102
1960	179.3 M	~87%	~10.5%	<4%	~1%	101.5
1970	203.2 M	~83%	~11%	~5%	~2%	101
1980	226.5 M	~80%	~11.7%	~6.5%	~3%	101.2
1990	248.7 M	~75%	~12%	~9%	~4%	100
2000	281.4 M	~69%	~12.3%	~12.5%	~5%	98.8
2010	309.3 M	~64%	~12.6%	~16%	~6%	98.6
2020	331.4 M	~58%	~12.1%	~18.7%	~10%**	98.8
2026(p)	~349 M***	~55%	~12.5%	~20%	~12%**	99.5

Note: In 1950, many Hispanics were classified as White.

Note: 2020+ includes "Two or more races" (~4%) in other categories.

Note: (p) denotes projections.

Note that the political and corporate leadership in the US more accurately reflects the population demographics of 1950 than 2026. As our population ages, and a younger, more diverse population is being elected to local, state, and national offices. As corporate leader age, the younger more diverse pool of employees are being promoted to leadership positions. The power shift is inevitable.

Where do you see yourself in this changing of demographics? Are you holding onto the values and implicate biases of the 1950's or growing to the reality of the demographics of 2026and beyond.

Growth and Migration Trends
U.S. population growth has slowed significantly, increasing by only **0.5%** (1.8 million people) between mid-2024 and mid-2025. (From the US Census Bureau.)

> **Migration Decline:** Net international migration dropped from a peak of 2.7 million in 2024 to 1.3 million in 2025. Projections for 2026 suggest it could decline further to approximately **321,000 to 570,000** people due to administrative actions and increased emigration. This decline in migration to the US will have a negative impact on our tax base and our ability to maintain vital infrastructure.

> **Fertility Rate:** The total fertility rate is projected to be **1.58 to 1.63** births per

woman in 2026, which is below the replacement rate of 2.1. This means each woman should give birth to 2 or more children to maintain the replacement rate of our current population. New immigrants to the US are more often younger, and give birth to more children than current US citizens. We need new immigrants to grow the population of this country.

Age and Race Demographics

The U.S. population is steadily aging, with the **65 and older** group growing faster than any other age bracket.

➢ **Aging Population:** The number of people age 65+ is projected to grow at an average annual rate of 1.6% through 2036, while the population age 24 or younger is expected to decline annually for the next 30 years.

➢ **Racial Composition (Recent Estimates):**

➢ **Non-Hispanic White:** ~57.6% to 58%. This group is experiencing a slight annual decline (roughly 0.2%) due to natural decrease (more deaths than births).

> **Hispanic/Latino:** ~19.1%, the fastest-growing major ethnic group with 1.2% annual growth.
> **Black/African American:** ~14.0%.
> **Asian:** ~6%, with growth primarily driven by international migration.
> **Two or More Races:** ~4.1%.

Regional Shifts

Recent data from January 2026 indicates that **South Carolina** is the fastest-growing state, followed by Idaho and North Carolina. Conversely, population declines have been noted in **California, Hawaii, New Mexico, Vermont, and West Virginia**. Florida has seen a sharp decrease in domestic migration, with only 22,517 people moving in during the latest period compared to over 310,000 in 2022, a decline of about 287,483 people per year.

US Demographics under age 25.

As of January 2026, Americans under the age of 25 represent a vital but shrinking portion of the total population, characterized by high racial diversity and a looming "demographic cliff."

Population Size and Share

➢ **Total Count:** Approximately **104.5 million** people are under age 25.

➢ **Population Share:** This group makes up roughly **30% to 35%** of the total U.S. population.

➢ **Decline Trend:** The population age 24 or younger is projected to decline annually by **0.8%** for the next 30 years due to historic lows in fertility rates.

Racial and Ethnic Diversity

Younger Americans are significantly more diverse than the overall population:

➢ **Minority Majority:** For the first time, youth under age 18 are "minority white," with minorities outnumbering non-Hispanic whites.

➢ **Breakdown (Ages 18–24):**

➢ **White (non-Hispanic):** 52%.

- ➢ **Hispanic/Latino:** 24% (the fastest-growing youth segment).
- ➢ **Black/African American:** 14%.
- ➢ **Asian:** 6%.
- ➢ **Multiracial:** 4%.
- ➢ **Immigrant Households:** More than **1 in 5** (22%) young people ages 14–24 are immigrants or live with at least one foreign-born parent.

Key Sub-Groups (2026 Estimates)

Age Group	Estimated Population	Key Characteristics
0–14 years	~60.6 million	Share of total population is ~17.3%.
15–19 years	~21.8 million	High school and early college age.
20–24 years	~21.5 million	Entering the workforce or finishing higher education.

Emerging "Demographic Cliff"

A significant drop-off in the number of 18-year-olds is projected to begin in **2026,** falling roughly **7.4%** by 2030. This trend is primarily driven by the "birth dearth" that started during the 2008 Great Recession and is expected to impact college enrollment and entry-level labor markets for years to come.

The US demographics of people under 20. As of January 2026, the U.S. population under 20 is approximately **83 million**, making up roughly **24–25%** of the total population. This segment is the most racially and ethnically diverse age group in the country, but it is also the only age bracket currently experiencing a steady decline in its total population share.

Therefore, state and federal government leaders, along with all corporations operating in the US, should recognize that your constituency and your customer base has already changed. New, first-time voters, are representing every social and ethic group in the US.   The upcoming 2028 national elections will include mostly non-white voters. They are alive and being educated in this country. And yes, they are citizens. If a political party wants to win elections in the future, they must include all minorities in the US.

They must also recognize that US electorate will be made up of minority voters since no single race will represent over 50% of our population. We should also understand that more and more US citizens are claiming their mixed heritage and self-identifying, not as white or African-Americas/Black, or Asian, but as Mixed or other.

Population Breakdown by Age
The latest estimates from the U.S. Census Bureau and KIDS COUNT Data Center divide this group as follows:
- **Ages 0–4:** ~18.5 million (Experiencing the largest decline of 8.2% since 2010).
- **Ages 5–14:** ~42.3 million.
- **Ages 15–19:** ~22.2 million.

Racial & Ethnic Diversity
For the first time in modern history, the population under age 20 is **"minority-**

majority," with racial and ethnic minorities accounting for over half of this age group.

> **Non-Hispanic White:** ~47–49%.
> **Hispanic/Latino:** ~26% (The fastest-growing youth segment, up from 9% in 1980).
> **Black/African American:** ~13.5–14%.
> **Asian:** ~5.5–6%.
> **Multiracial:** ~4–5%.

Key Demographic Trends for 2026

> **Shrinking Youth Population:** While the overall U.S. population is growing, the under-20 population is declining due to a falling birth rate and a shrinking pool of women in childbearing years.
> **Immigrant Households:** Approximately **25%** of all children under 18 in the U.S. are first- or second-generation immigrants, living with at least one foreign-born parent.
> **Geographic Growth Pockets:** Despite the national decline, the under-20 population is actually **growing** in states like **Texas and Florida** due to high rates of domestic and international migration.

➤ **Language:** Roughly **21%** of children ages 5–17 do not speak English at home, though only about 5% report having difficulty with the language.

Please recognize that most people share DNA with multiple groups even though they may self-identify as one primary race or ethnicity. Which race and/or ethnicity do you choose for yourself? Do you think that any of the races listed are better than others?

What are you going to do to improve relations with members of each demographic group in the United States?

In summary, we are experiencing the Browning of America.

Pop Quiz – Who Lives in the United States in 2026?

#	Question	Yes	No
1	Do you understand that the citizens of the United States are the decedents of American Indians, Mexican Americans, Europeans, African Americans, Pacific Islanders, and others from around the world?		
2	Do you understand that by the next election cycle, about 50% of this country will be non-white and how this effect you?		
3	Do you believe each person in this country is entitled to being treated with dignity and respect, including you and your family members, regardless of race, creed, religion, sex, or country of national origin?		
4	Do you believe the US should modify our immigration laws to welcome and quickly integrate people into the US with work permits and permanent resident status?		
5	Should the US government utilize immigration enforcement practices that are non-combative and respectful to immigrants, citizens, employers, and the general public?		

5 "Love Thy Neighbor as Thyself."

Your view of neighbors, affects your view of the world. If you consider someone a neighbor, you/we are more likely to support that neighbor in a crisis. If you/we don't consider them a neighbor, we are more likely to turn our backs on them when they are in need. The definition of neighbor influences our views and actions in our laws, emergency services, defense spending, and our attitude about how we fit into the world. Your definition of neighbor will likely determine if you will "Love or Hate, or Ignore" other human beings. Your definition of "neighbor" influences your view of people in your community, state, nation, and even your world view. Let's take a deep dive into the phase, to better understand ow you really think.

More importantly, your community's definition of neighbor will influence the structure and intent of laws. Your community's definition of neighbor will likely influence or determine how laws are administered to people. Sentences for crimes committed by neighbors tend to be much lighter than sentences for "non-neighbors", "strangers", who are commonly referred to as "those people."

Let's examine if you really "Love thy neighbor as thyself."

The essence of this message has been implemented into societies worldwide. Many of the laws of the Unites States and countries on every continent include this sentiment. The question in this chapter is, "Do you live practice the essence of this message in your daily life?" This answer will assist you in answering the primary question in this book about yourself. "Who am I in 2025".

The historical origin of this phase can be traced to the Quran, the Torah, and the Christian Bible. This is a core principle of Judaism, Islam, Hindu, Buddhism and Christianity and a common sentiment across many religions worldwide. Let's review where the phase appears in each of the three major religions.

This phase is from the Christian bible: The phrase "Love thy neighbor as thyself" appears in Leviticus 19:18 in the Old Testament, and is also quoted by Jesus in the New Testament in Matthew 22:39, Mark 12:31, and Luke 10:27, where He identifies it as the second greatest commandment.

In Islam, a similar principle is found in the saying, "Not one of you truly believes until you wish for others what you wish for yourself," which promotes altruism and empathy towards one's fellow human beings. This is from the Quran 4:34.

In Hebrew, the phrase "Love thy neighbor as thyself" is in the Torah, specifically in Leviticus 19:18. This verse is a foundational commandment of Jewish ethics, interpreted as a central principle of the Torah that encourages kindness, generosity, and moral responsibility towards others.

While, the concept of "Love thy neighbor as thyself" is not directly found as a quote in Hindu scriptures, its closest equivalent is the principle of treating others as one wishes to be treated, as found in the ancient Hitopadesh and the Mahabharata.

A core Hindu metaphysical teaching, Tat Tvam Asi ("Thou Art That"), also provides a philosophical foundation for this concept by positing the unity of all beings, suggesting a deeper reason to love others as oneself because they are, in essence, a part of the self.

Buddhism does not have a single "holy book" but rather a vast collection of scriptures called the Tripitaka (or Tipitaka),

meaning "Three Baskets". This collection is
the core of Buddhist teachings and is
divided into three main sections: the Vinaya
Pitaka (discipline), Sutta Pitaka (discourses),
and Abhidhamma Pitaka (doctrine).

When you dial 911 to request emergency services, do you welcome the first responders or make a special request for first responders of your ethnicity, age, political affiliation?

Most 911 callers want immediate support, regardless of demographic group.

Different Buddhist traditions also have
additional sutras and tantras within their
own canons. The Tripitaka does not contain
the exact phrase "Love thy neighbor as
thyself," which is a Christian teaching, but it
does teach a similar concept of universal
loving-kindness (Metta) through phrases like
"Hurt not others in ways that you yourself
would find hurtful" and the Karaniya Metta
Sutta, which encourages wishing all beings
to be at ease.

Now we see that the essence of the message
is the same in multiple religions worldwide.

Therefor we can conclude that, "Love thy neighbor as thyself", is a foundational tenant of humanity, regardless of faith, or nationality. Therefore, do you practice this tenant is most aspects of your life when dealing with other people?

Consider the following. What can you do to have a more inclusive definition of neighbor? How can you support that more inclusive definition? Can you show an act of kindness to your neighbors daily? Can you introduce yourself and develop a positive relationship with new neighbors?

<u>What is the meaning of "Neighbor?"</u>

Most dictionaries define "Neighbor" as someone who lives nearby. The expanded definition includes "fellow Man (or woman). I encourage you to adopt the definition that specifies "fellow man/woman.

Historically, people of similar background chose to live near each other. In cities, neighbor hoods, sometimes referred to as ghettos, were populated with people who shared a common background. In many towns and cities, people in one neighborhood considered people from another neighborhood as strangers, therefore they must be troublemakers. Therefore, all strangers were treated with distrust, fear, and harshness. Definition of stranger. A person who is not known in a place or community.

Note that at any given moment, in any group of people, you will be look upon as a neighbor or stranger. How do you prefer being viewed by others? How do you treat others?

After answering the questions below, consider your answers. Do you really "Love thy neighbor as thyself?" If you want to be treated well by others, are you willing to treat others well?

Pop Quiz - "Love Thy Neighbor as Thyself."

#	Question	Yes	No
1	Do you recognize most people who live in your town/city/county as your neighbor?		
2	If and when a neighbor gets in trouble with the law and is charged with a minor crime, should the courts show leniency?		
3	If and when a stranger/ immigrant gets in trouble with the law and is charged with a minor crime, should the courts show leniency?		
4	In time of natural disasters, do you offer assistance to those in need, regardless of neighbor status?		
5	When you are in need, do you expect your neighbors to show you compassions and provide assistance?		

6 Do you believe in the Caste system?

If you truly believe that each person is equal, then you don't believe in the caste system. However, if you support laws that are applied more harshly to "those people" than to your people, you might be supporting a Caste system. If you look down on a group of people, you might be supporting a Caste system. Let's explore this concept and determine what you believe in and how you act.

If you were raised being taught that you were better or less than other groups of people, you have been raised in a Caste system. In the United States there is no official Caste system, however, there is an unofficial system in place. The unofficial Caste system has influenced our laws and how we apply those laws. It also has influenced how we view each other.

The Constitution of the United States was allegedly written to make each person equal. The 27 Amendments to the US Constitution made it clear that all people in the US, regardless of race, sex, national origin, or religion, were to be considered equal and were to be treated equally under the law. The intent was to create a society where the system of Kings, feudal lords, and peasants was eliminated. The goal was to create a society where each person was free and could create the career and life style that they sought, regardless of your position at birth.

However, many US citizens know that we, the people of this country, missed the mark.

Only we the people of the United States can change this system. Now the most important questions of all. Are you willing to challenge and change the US Caste system to make this a better country? Are you willing to open your eyes, see injustices, and take peaceful corrective action? Are you willing to become politically active to eliminate the caste system?

If you were raised being taught that you were better or less than other groups of people, you have been raised in a Caste system.

North America was inhabited by native peoples beginning around 30,000 to 20,000 years ago. They lived in harmony with the land. As the population grew and expanded throughout North and South America, they continued to live in harmony. There was no Caste system.

Then European settlers came to the Americas in the 1600s. They left a system of life based largely on the Monarchy, feudal Lord, and peasant system. This was an extreme Caste system.
The society developed in the United States, by Europeans was designed for equality for all, but was heavily influenced by their common experiences. Women, American Indians, African Slaves, and Asian immigrants were not included in the definition of "all".

While the U.S. Constitution was written to support equality for all, many federal, state, and local laws were written with significant bias against a selected group of people. Basically, we the people of the United States built a Caste system through various laws. The criminal justice system supported the Caste system by applying laws in such a manner as to favor or discriminate against a group of people.

Have you been taught to see people through the lens of a hierarchical ranking, a Caste System? Do you mentally judge people or assign value to them based on a value system based in part on a Caste system? The answer to these questions will shed a light on why you see the world the way you do and why you have bias to or for selected group of people.

Let's define the CASTE system. Three models are explained below. The US Caste system, the Indian Caste, and Spanish Casta Colonial system.

United States Caste System

While the term "caste system" isn't a formal legal structure in the U.S., many scholars argue that the United States operates under a de facto caste system rooted in race, particularly for white and Black Americans. This system, described in Isabel Wilkerson's book Caste, functions as an ingrained social hierarchy based on inherited status, distributing power and privilege based on perceived bloodline or race, rather than solely on individual merit.

This Caste System was developed by White European immigrants to North Americas beginning in the 1600. Of course they put themselves at the top of the Caste System. They also developed a Caste System where individuals could not move up or down the Caste ranking system. Therefore, the system implies that you don't need to try to move up because you will never be accepted.

Origins and Foundations
➢ Slavery:

The U.S. caste system has deep roots in the centuries-long institution of slavery, which legally and socially positioned people of African descent as a permanent underclass.

➢ Race as a Visible Cue:
In this system, race serves as the visible marker that assigns individuals to their designated caste, with white people forming the dominant caste and Black people the subordinate caste.

Characteristics of the American Caste System

➢ Graded Hierarchy:

It's a fixed ranking of human value, with the dominant caste at the top and others ranked in descending order, often based on their proximity to the dominant group.

➢ Systemic Inequality:

Caste status determines social, political, and economic opportunities and expectations, perpetuating disparities in areas like housing, healthcare, and education.

➢ Hereditary Transmission:

Caste status is inherited through generations, meaning that individuals are born into their societal rank, and societal positions are fixed regardless of individual achievement.

➢ Endogamy:

A system that discourages or prohibits relationships and marriages between people of different castes.

Impact and Manifestations

➢ Institutional Racism:

The legacy of the American caste system is evident in pervasive racial disparities and systemic inequalities that persist today, such as disproportionate police brutality against Black individuals.

➢ Social and Political Division:

The system continues to influence present-day divisions along social, political, and economic lines, even as society changes.

➢ Global Resonance:
While distinct, the U.S. system is discussed alongside other global caste-based systems, including those in India, to understand the universal nature of such rigid social stratifications.

Unofficial Caste System Chart for the USA

Dominant Caste - White People

Middle Caste - People who are neither white or Black - Asains Americans, Native Americans, mixed race and other groups.

Subordinate Caste - Black People, Africans, Carribean Islanders

New Subordinate Class Members - 1970 - present day new Immagrants - Latinos, Muslims, Africans

Source - Isabel Wilkerson

Drawing a simple, definitive diagram of a "caste system" for the United States is not possible because the concept itself is a subject of academic debate. While the U.S. does not have an officially recognized caste system like the historical one in India, author Isabel Wilkerson and other scholars argue that a similar, race-based social hierarchy has long functioned as the country's hidden infrastructure.

Instead of a single diagram, the American social hierarchy can be represented through two main lenses:
➢ A race-based caste model, as proposed by Isabel Wilkerson.

➢ A multi-factor social stratification model, which is the more traditional sociological view.

In her Pulitzer Prize-winning book *Caste: The Origins of Our Discontents*, Isabel Wilkerson argues that the U.S. operates under an unacknowledged caste system. She asserts that race is the "visible skin," while caste is the "invisible skeleton" of American social hierarchy.
Diagram of Wilkerson's U.S. caste system. The model primarily uses a two-tiered system based on race, with a smaller "middle caste" occupying an intermediary space.

I have expanded the model to include immigrants to the US, who arrived in this country after the Vietnam/ American war, US/Afghanistan Way, the aftermath of September 11, 2001, and more recent unrest in Central and South America, and Africa.

Dominant Caste: "White" people
➢ Historically holds the highest social standing, privilege, and access to resources.

➢ Has been socialized into a sense of entitlement and has historically resisted efforts by the subordinate caste to gain equality.

Middle Caste: People who are not "white" or "Black"
➢ Includes Asian Americans, Native Americans, and other groups.

➢ Historically navigated the bipolar system, often subject to distinct forms of discrimination.

➢ Is often used by the dominant caste as a buffer or to reinforce the hierarchy.

➢ Subordinate Caste: "Black" people
➢ Holds the lowest position in the hierarchy, with its origins tied to slavery.

➢ Suffers disproportionately from systemic disadvantages in employment opportunities, housing, education, wealth, and criminal justice.

New Subordinate Class Members – from 1970 - present day includes new Immigrants - Latinos, Muslims, Africans
➢ Holds the lowest of low position in the hierarchy, with its origins tied to the aftermath of wars and terrorist acts.

➢ Suffers disproportionately from systemic disadvantages in employment opportunities, housing, education, wealth, and criminal justice.

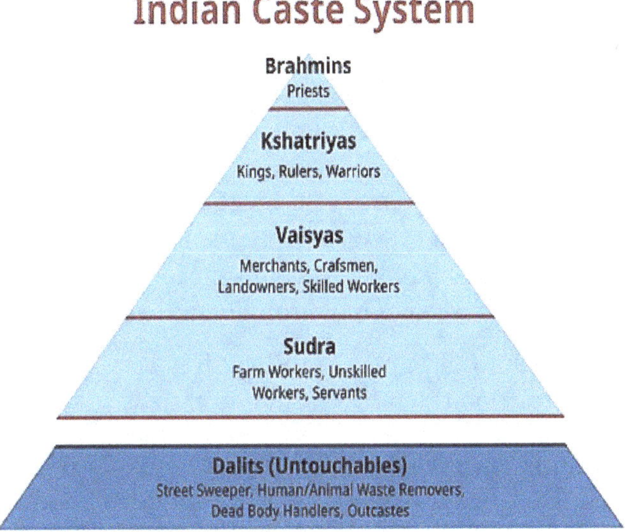

Source Wikipedia

Indian Caste System

A caste system is a rigid, hereditary social hierarchy where a person's social status, opportunities, and way of life are determined by their birth, not personal merit. These systems create closed social groups with strict rules about marriage (endogamy) and social interactions, limiting social mobility between castes.

<u>Cast structure</u>

- Brahmins = Priests
- Kshatriyas = Kings, Rulers, & Warriors
- Vaisyas = Merchants, craftsmen, landowners, & Skilled workers
- Sundra = Farm Workers, Unskilled workers, & farmers
- Dalits (Untouchables) = Street sweeper, human and animal waste removers, dead body handlers, & outcasts

<u>Key Characteristics of a Caste System</u>

- **Hereditary Status:** A person's place in the social hierarchy is assigned at birth and passed down through families.

- **Limited Social Mobility:** It is very difficult to move from one caste to another, as positions are fixed by heredity.

- **Endogamy:** Individuals typically marry within their own caste.

- **Occupational Restrictions:** Occupations are often inherited, with people born into specific roles.

- **Social and Cultural Barriers:** There are often restrictions on social interaction between castes, including rules about eating together and physical contact.

- **Hierarchy:** The system is hierarchical, with different castes positioned at various levels of social status and power.

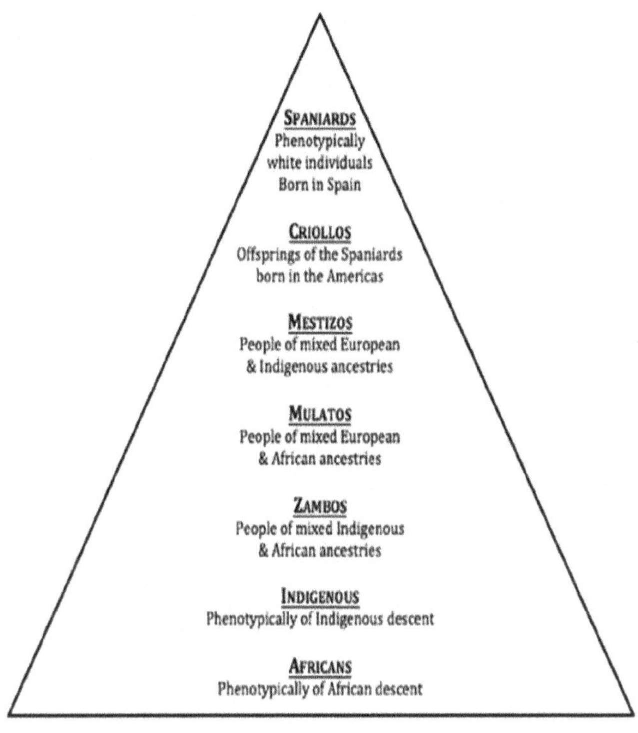

Latin American Social Caste Pyramid (LASCP).

Spanish Casta Colonial system

The Casta system was a Spanish colonial social hierarchy in Mexico that classified people by race and ancestry, granting different rights, status, and opportunities based on their perceived "blood purity". At the top were people born in Spain (Peninsulares), followed by Spaniards born in the Americas (Criollos), then mixed-race categories like Mestizos (Spanish and Indigenous) and Mulattoes (Spanish and African), with Indigenous people and Africans at the bottom. This rigid system, visually depicted in casta paintings, aimed to maintain Spanish dominance and has left a lasting legacy of color hierarchy and racial discrimination in Mexico today.

Clearly this Casta system was written by the Spanish born individuals who financed the expeditions to the Americas. In this system, equality for all was unachievable.

Key Aspects of the Casta System
- Racial Hierarchy:

  Individuals were categorized into complex racial classifications based on their presumed mixture of Spanish, Indigenous, and African ancestry.

- Social & Economic Status:

  One's casta designation significantly affected social status, access to education, and employment opportunities.

- Spanish Control:
  The system served to maintain Spanish power by creating a rigid social order and reinforcing cultural hierarchies.

Las castas. A casta painting showing 16 racial groupings. Anonymous, 18th century, oil on canvas, 148×104 cm, Museo Nacional del Virreinato, Tepotzotlán, Mexico

Wikipedia Las Casta Painting

Examples of Casta
- ➢ Peninsulares: Spaniards born in Spain.
- ➢ Criollos: Spaniards born in the
- ➢ Americas.
- ➢ Mestizos: People of mixed Spanish and Indigenous ancestry.
- ➢ Mulattoes: People of mixed Spanish and African ancestry.
- ➢ Indigenous Peoples: Native Americans.

➢ Africans: People of African descent.

Lasting Impacts
➢ Color Hierarchy:

The system created a color hierarchy where those perceived as "whiter" generally have higher social status and more opportunities, a phenomenon that persists today.

➢ Discrimination:
The legacy of the Casta system contributes to present-day discrimination based on skin color in areas like employment and education.

Pop Quiz - "The Casta System"

#	Question	Yes	No
1	Do you think you are better than other people in this country based on race, religion, sexual orientation?		
2	Have you been taught by your parents and loved one to distrust people who are not from your community, based on a caste system?		
3	Do you believe in financial hierarchy? I.e. Rich people are better and smarter than poorer people?		
4	Do you have a bias against any group of people, based on race, sex, country of origin, sexual orientation, immigration status?		
5	Could you survive and prosper in this country if you were suddenly reassigned from the top to the bottom of the Caste system?		

7 Moral Crisis of the US Immigration System

From 1892 to 1954, the US welcomed new European immigrants to the United States. After passing a health screening at their point of entry, (such as Ellis Island), most immigrants were welcomed to the US with full rights to work and contribute to society. Most were authorized to apply for citizenship after the required waiting periods and educational requirements. More than 12,000,000 people immigrated to the US through Ellis Island. But oh, how the US immigration policies have changed.

The current United States immigration system is frequently criticized for institutionalizing inequities that disproportionately impact marginalized groups based on race, nationality, and economic status. The current immigration system in the US forces most immigrants into economic slavery by restricting their ability to legally work in this country. Without a tax id number and the legal authorization to work, employers cannot legally hire immigrants. Therefore, immigrants are forced into some form of illegal work, otherwise known economic slavery. As of 2026, these disparities have been sharpened by new legislative and executive actions that restrict access to legal pathways and public benefits.

However, in 2026 the US view on immigration has changed for the worst. We have about 4.27% of the world's population of 8 billion people, yet we imprison, detain, and hold more immigrants than anywhere else in the world. Is this who we are? Who benefits from this system of mass detention and deportation? Why is the United States immigration system looking more and more like the World War II German concentration camp system? If this information is alarming to you, what are you going to do about it? Sitting on the sidelines is not an option.

The current immigration system in the United States prevents many immigrants from getting work authorizations and thus creates an economic slavery system. People without work permits are forced to work "under the table", meaning without proper federal and state tax id numbers. Employer's often take advantage of undocumented workers, by not paying them, holding their passports, charging exorbitant rates for living expenses, and human trafficking.

The United States operates the world's largest immigration detention system.

As of late 2025/early 2026, the United States operates the world's largest immigration detention system, with U.S. Immigration and Customs Enforcement (ICE) utilizing over 200 to 300+ facilities (including jails, prisons, and private centers) to detain immigrants. Daily detained populations recently exceeded 50,000 individuals, with Texas, Louisiana, California, and Georgia housing the highest numbers.

Key Details on Detention Facilities (2025-2026):

- **Capacity & Usage:** By late 2025, ICE reported using over 100 more facilities compared to the start of the year.

- **Facility Types:** These include ICE-owned service processing centers, contract detention facilities (private), and over 200 state and local jails or juvenile centers.

- **Daily Populations:** As of June 1, 2025, over 51,000 people were in ICE detention.

- **Largest Facilities:** The Adams County Detention Center in Mississippi holds over 2,000 people.

Racial Disparities in Enforcement and Processing

Racial inequity remains a foundational issue within the system. Research indicates that while immigration from Europe has historically been met with pathways toward integration, immigrants of color face systemic barriers.

- **Deportation Trends:** Black immigrants, despite representing a small fraction of the noncitizen population, have historically faced a <u>disproportionately high rate</u> of deportation proceedings. Immigrants from Caribbean Nations, Central and South American Nations, Africa, and India have a high deportation rate.

- **Asylum Access:** As of early 2026, U.S. Citizenship and Immigration Services (USCIS) has implemented an indefinite pause on asylum adjudications for nationals from specific "high-risk" countries, significantly impacting applicants from various African and Middle Eastern nations.

- **Differential Treatment:** Policies often apply harsher consequences for unauthorized entry to Latino and Black immigrants than to white immigrants for similar offenses.

Economic and Wealth-Based Barriers
The system increasingly prioritizes high-wealth individuals, creating a "pay-to-play" environment that excludes lower-income workers.

- **New Fees:** A 2025 presidential proclamation introduced a $100,000 fee for new H-1B visa petitions for workers outside the U.S., effectively barring smaller businesses and nonprofits from recruiting specialized talent. Additionally, a new $250 "Visa Integrity Fee" applies to most nonimmigrant categories starting in 2026. A point to consider is that a wealthy individual with $100,000 to pay the 1B fee would be volunteering for economic slavery by their US employer. If you have earned and saved $100,000 in your home country, you likely do not need a job in the US.

- Wage-Based Lottery: The H-1B lottery has shifted to a weighted system that gives higher-paid applicants (Level 4 wage) four times the chance of selection compared to Level 1 applicants, disadvantaging lower-paying sectors like healthcare and research.

- Financial Vulnerability: Approximately 50% of immigrants in late 2025 reported struggling to pay for basic needs like housing and food, up from 31% in 2023.

Institutional and Legal Inequities

Administrative changes in 2025 and 2026 have reduced the "due process" available to noncitizens.

- Reduction in Work Authorization: The validity period for Employment Authorization Documents (EADs) was cut from five years to just 18 months, increasing the financial and administrative burden on refugees and asylum seekers who must now renew more frequently.

- Visa Halts: In January 2026, the Department of State halted immigrant visa processing for nationals of 75 countries, citing security and public benefit concerns.

- Public Benefit Restrictions: New budget laws starting in 2026 eliminate Medicaid and CHIP funding for certain noncitizens, including refugees and asylees, further deepening health inequities.

Impact on Future Generations

Inequity extends to the children of immigrants, many of whom are U.S. citizens.

- Mental Health: Legal precarity and the constant fear of parental deportation contribute to high rates of PTSD, anxiety, and developmental delays among immigrant children.

- Educational Barriers: Undocumented high school graduates face declining access to tuition equity and higher education programs, undermining their long-term economic mobility.

The US needs new Immigrants. The United States benefits significantly from new immigrants migrating to the country through various economic and social channels. These benefits include addressing labor shortages, fostering economic growth, and driving innovation and entrepreneurship.

Economic Growth and Labor Force

➢ Meeting Labor Demands: Immigration helps provide for current and growing labor needs across various industries. Analysis suggests that raising immigration levels annually could increase the projected U.S. working-age population by about 13% by 2040, which further expands the U.S. economy.

➢ Alleviating Inflation: By easing worker shortages, increased immigration can help drive down inflation and consumer prices.

➢ Significant Contributions: Immigrants make substantial contributions to the U.S. economy, including ensuring that essential services continue to be provided across the country.

➢ Entrepreneurship and Innovation

➢ Founding Businesses: Immigrants are more likely to found firms of all sizes compared to native-born individuals, with a higher percentage engaging in entrepreneurship. This creates jobs and stimulates economic activity.

➢ Major Companies: Immigrants have founded or co-founded many major American corporations. New American Fortune 500 companies generated more than \$7 trillion in revenue in fiscal year 2021, a figure greater than the GDP of many developed countries.

➢ Social and Individual Benefits

➢ Stability and Opportunity: Creating a pathway to citizenship for undocumented immigrants increases stability for them and their families, translating to better educational and employment opportunities, which ultimately benefits the broader society and economy.

By fixing our damaged immigration system, we will benefit from having legal workers who are contributing to our tax base.

Counter Balances a Low Birth Rate: The U.S. birth rate has dropped to record lows, falling to approximately 1.6 births per woman by 2024–2025, well below the 2.1 "replacement rate" needed to maintain population stability. This long-term, downward trend is driven by economic, social, and structural factors, including high costs of child care, student debt, and delayed childbearing. Immigration increases the population of this country.

Immigration serves as a crucial, and often primary, driver of population and labor force growth in the United States, directly offsetting the demographic, economic, and fiscal challenges caused by the nation's low birth rate, which has remained below the replacement level of 2.1 children per woman for years. Here is an explanation of how immigration counterbalances the low birth rate in the US:

Direct Population Growth

➢ Replacing Declining Natural Increase: With US fertility rates below replacement, the gap between births and deaths has narrowed. Immigration has become the primary driver of US population growth, accounting for roughly 80% of total growth in recent years.

➢ Short-term Fix for Aging: Immigration introduces a younger, working-age population, which helps balance the demographic profile as the native-born population ages and moves into retirement.

➢ Future Projections: The Congressional Budget Office (CBO) projects that as native births continue to decline, net immigration will be essential to keeping the US population from shrinking by 2030–2033.

Economic and Labor Force Support

➢ Expanding the Working-Age Population: Immigrants often fill labor shortages, particularly in industries requiring both high-skilled and lower-skilled labor.

➢ Supporting Social Safety Nets: By contributing to the tax base, working-age immigrants help support social insurance programs like Social Security and Medicare, which face strain from an aging, retired population.

➢ Economic Stimulus: Recent surges in immigration have been linked to robust job growth, providing labor and generating demand for goods and services.

Impact on Fertility Rates

➢ Higher Fertility Rates: Generally, immigrant women in the US have a higher total fertility rate (TFR) than native-born women (e.g., 2.19 for immigrants vs. 1.73 for native-born in 2023).

➢ Slight Boost to Overall TFR: While immigrant fertility has declined, the presence of immigrants still raises the overall national TFR, contributing to a higher total number of births.

Directing Demographic Momentum
➢ Countering the "Baby Dearth": Without immigration, the US would face a much faster, steeper, and more immediate decline in population, similar to situations seen in other developed nations.

➢ Regional Rejuvenation: Immigrants often settle in areas with rapidly aging populations, helping to rejuvenate local communities and keep schools and local economies active.

Key Considerations and Limitations
➢ While immigration helps, it is not a complete solution to the demographic shift:
➢ Declining Immigrant Fertility: Immigrant fertility rates have also declined over time, as they often

adopt lower birth-rate patterns after arriving in the US.

➢ Small Impact on Total TFR: The overall impact of immigration on the total fertility rate is relatively small raising the total TFR by only a fraction (e.g., from 1.73 for natives to 1.80 for the total population in 2023).

➢ Indirect Effects on Native Fertility: Some research indicates that, in certain areas, high levels of immigration may coincide with higher housing costs or job competition, which can indirectly depress the fertility rate of native-born residents.

In summary, immigration provides immediate, necessary support for the US population and labor force, acting as a crucial counterweight to the demographic challenges posed by low fertility. Additionally, new immigrants are integral to the U.S. economy, filling crucial labor gaps, boosting entrepreneurship, and contributing significantly to the nation's overall economic prosperity.

By fixing our damaged immigration system, we will minimize, economic slavery and reduce the need for detention centers. We will benefit from having legal workers who pay taxes and are contributing to our tax base. More information can be found at the "Center for American Progress, Kellogg Insight, and FWD.US.

Pop Quiz - "Moral Crisis of the Immigration System"

#	Question	Yes	No
1	Should the US implement immigration reforms that allow immigrants to settle in the US with permanent residency and work authorization immediately upon arrival, as we did prior to 1945?		
2	Should the US implement immigration reforms that allow immigrants regardless of race, religion, or country of national origin?		
3	Should US government's immigration control agencies, be prohibited from using heavy handed methods to enforce immigration laws?		
4	Should the officers within immigration enforcement agencies be held accountable for assaults and shootings of people?		
5	Can we, the people of the United States, do a better job of administering immigration laws, than we did in 2025 and 2026?		

8 Do you want "Win – Win" or "Win – Lose" Scenarios?

In 2025 and 2026, the USA created win-lose or lose-lose scenarios with most of our long-term allies and trading partners, through the implementation of import tariffs. This chapter asks you to decide if you want to live in a world where we the people in the USA create win-win or win-lose scenarios. Consider which condition is best for you personally, your family, your country, your income and savings, and our neighbors worldwide.

In our personal lives, Win-Win scenarios are experienced in dating, employment, housing and virtually every aspect of our lives. Each party feel they are receiving a fair and equitable return on their investment of time, energy, money, and emotions. Life is good. You treat people fairly and they return fair treatment to you. Win – Win Scenarios usually lead to long term "good will" between participants.

Examples of Win – Win scenarios

➢ In international trade, a win-win scenario occurs when two or more countries engage in voluntary exchange that leaves all parties better off than they were before. Economists generally view trade as a positive-sum game rather than a zero-sum game.

- ➤ In personal relationships, it is a friendship where each participant feels valued and appreciated.
- ➤ In love relationships, each person feels loved, safe, and secure in the committed relationship.
- ➤ In work relationships it means, fair pay for fair work contributions, career opportunities, upward mobility, and the creation and maintenance of a safe and equitable work environment.
- ➤ In travel and immigration matters, we expect quick and easy, access to visas and travel arrangements between countries, for vacations, work related activities, and to visit relatives.

In summary, a Win – Win scenario generates a fair and equitable outcome for each participant. It also generates trust and "good-will." Communities work better when there is trust due to fair and equitable relations among all parties.

<u>Now let's look at the Win-Loose scenario.</u>

A win-lose scenario is a distributive negotiation or conflict outcome where one party gains at the expense of another. It is characterized by competitive, adversarial, or zero-sum dynamics where one party's success requires the other's failure. This approach often leads to damaged long-term relationships and mistrust.

There are many examples of wealthy countries creating "win-lose" scenarios with countries they colonize. In these scenarios the colonizer usually levies an unfair deal with the weaker country and enforces that unfair advantage with a strong military presence. Colonizers also implement currency and financial management systems which ensure they will retain an unfair advantage. In all cases, the colony will eventually find a way out of the unfair win-lose scenario. Sometime this is accomplished peacefully. Unfortunately, this correction often requires war.

In 2025 and 2026, the government of the United States of America (USA), implemented a USA first agenda upon the world. The USA levied tariffs on 90 countries at the time of this writing. Most of the tariffs were levied in a seemingly retaliatory manner. The effect of the tariffs included the following.

- ➢ Increased prices for US importers and thus increased prices for US consumers.
- ➢ Disruption in international supply chains due to unpredictable prices of items.
- ➢ Generated "Ill will" (hostile feelings, malevolence, and distrust) with international trading partners.

➢ Trading partners found alternative sources for goods and services previously procured from the USA.

Once new fair and equitable international trade relationships are established, the participating countries will rarely return to the USA for decades. Once you lose a customer, you may lose that customer for decades.

Once the customers are lost, consider the effects of USA suppliers and producers. The implementation of high tariffs on USA trading partners had a negative effect.
➢ Foreign importers stopped or significantly reduced the import of agricultural products such as meats, poultry, and grain.
➢ Foreign suppliers developed new supply chains that excluded the USA.
➢ Higher consumer prices and inflation within the US.
➢ Trade Wars
➢ Reduced economic growth in the US.
➢ Strained international trade relations.

The third alternative is a Lose-lose scenario. This occurs when all parties sustain significant losses due to disagreements or conflicts. Everyone loses. Nobody wins. Example of lose-lose scenarios include the following.
➢ Military wars

> ➢ Trade wars including import and export tariffs
> ➢ Natural disasters
> ➢ Business deals gone bad
> ➢ Personal relationships gone bad

In summary, the world does not trust that the USA will be a stable international partner in trade, defense, humanitarianism, finance, and any global issues. Now, what can you do to improve living conditions inside the US? What can you do to improve international relations?

Pop Quiz - "Win-win, win-lose, or lose-lose scenario"

#	Question	Yes	No
1	Do you think US tariffs create a win-lose or lose-lose scenario?		
2	Has the "US first" attitude hurt international relations with US allies and trading partners?		
3	Will it take more than 5 years to reestablish good international trade relations and trust?		
4	Have tariffs hurt the US economy?		
5	Would you prefer to live in the USA with win-win international trade relations and win-win immigration reforms?		

9 The World is Divorcing the USA

For three generations following World War II, the United States of America served as the undisputed anchor of the global economic, political, and security system. This "rules-based order" was characterized by the dominance of the US dollar, the ubiquity of American pop culture, and reliance on the US military for stability. However, from 2016 - 2026, that landscape underwent a dramatic transformation.

Driven by a combination of, at times, erratic foreign policy ("America First" initiatives), the weaponization of economic sanctions, and the rise of alternative power centers, the world is increasingly "divorcing" the United States. This chapter will outline the mechanisms of this "divorce," analyzing the shift in trade, the erosion of the dollar's dominance, and the decline of US diplomatic authority.

**The Economic Divorce: De-dollarization
and Trade Realignment**

The most significant aspect of this global
shift is the systemic move away from the
U.S. dollar, often referred to as "de-
dollarization." By 2025, the dollar's share of
global foreign exchange reserves dropped to
around 58%, the lowest level in thirty years.

> **The Rise of Alternative
> Currencies:** Countries, particularly
> within the BRICS alliance (Brazil,
> Russia, India, China, South Africa), are
> accelerating the use of local currencies
> for cross-border trade. China and Russia
> now conduct over 55% of their bilateral
> trade in Chinese Yuan. India is settling
> oil purchases with the UAE and Russia
> using Indian Rupees and UAE Dirhams
> rather than US Dollars.

> **Weaponization of Finance:** The
> extensive use of sanctions—effectively
> freezing the dollar-denominated assets of
> Russia following the Ukraine conflict—
> has spurred many nations to seek

alternatives to avoid similar risks. This has prompted a surge in central bank purchasing of gold as a "safe haven" asset, which reached record levels in 2024–2025.

➢ **Trading Away from America:** The U.S. has seen its trading partnerships strained due to protectionist trade policies and tariffs, leading allies and adversaries alike to seek new trade pacts. For instance, Canada has begun moving away from being exclusively tied to the U.S. market, with Canadian vehicle imports from Mexico surpassing those from the U.S. in 2025. Additionally, major economic deals, such as the 2026 India-EU agreement, are moving forward without U.S. participation.

The Geopolitical Divorce: Shifting Alliances

The "divorce" is not limited to economics; it extends to a major realignment of geopolitical power, where countries are seeking to distance themselves from

American foreign policy, which is often viewed as unstable or self-interested.

> **The Rise of Alternative Power Hubs:** As the U.S. reduces its commitment to global leadership and international institutions, China is rapidly filling the void. Beijing has taken a more active role in mediating global conflicts and providing alternative economic development paths through the Belt and Road Initiative.

> **Loss of Trust and Influence:** Favorable European views of the U.S. dropped by nearly 13% between 2024 and 2025, signaling a decline in "soft power". Nations in the Global South, as well as some traditional European allies, are adopting a more "non-aligned" stance, refusing to be caught between the U.S. and China.

> **Withdrawal from International Institutions:** The U.S. has, at times, withdrawn from international bodies, such as the World Health Organization (WHO), treating international

cooperation as a zero-sum game. This withdrawal has allowed other nations to step into leadership roles, eroding American influence in setting global health and, by extension, economic standards.

The Diplomatic Divorce: "America First" and Isolation

The "America First" policy approach has created a perception of the U.S. as an unreliable partner, leading to a "divorce" in diplomatic trust.

➢ **Tariff Wars and Retaliation:** The imposition of tariffs on allies, such as Canada and European nations, has spurred retaliation. This has not only affected trade volumes but has also damaged the long-standing political alliances that once underpinned U.S. global influence.

➢ **The "Erratic" Foreign Policy Paradigm:** The unpredictability of U.S. foreign policy has encouraged nations to diversify their security alliances. When allies cannot rely on the United States to honor its commitments, they seek alternative security arrangements or develop independent capabilities, effectively divorcing their security interests from Washington.

Consequences for the United States

This global divorce has serious implications for the American economy and its role in the world.

- ➢ **The Cost of "Divorce":** As the world reduces its reliance on the dollar, the U.S. may no longer be able to finance its massive debt (surpassing $37 trillion in 2025) as cheaply. A decline in demand for U.S. Treasuries could drive up interest rates, forcing Americans to pay more for borrowing and potentially leading to higher inflation.

- ➢ **Reduced Economic Influence:** If countries are less reliant on the US dollar and American markets, US sanctions become less effective. This weakens the primary tool the U.S. uses to enforce its foreign policy objectives.

- ➤ **The End of American Exceptionalism:** The "divorce" signifies a shift from a unipolar world (dominated by the US) to a multipolar world. The United States will be forced to operate as one of several major powers rather than the hegemon. This could mean a significant decline in the American standard of living as the economic benefits of being the world's reserve currency provider diminish.

Conclusion

The "divorce" of the world from the United States is not a single, sudden event, but a gradual process of decoupling. It is driven by a desire among nations for greater autonomy, fear of American financial sanctions, and the search for more stable, regional, or multipolar power structures. While the U.S. still holds the largest economy, its position as the undisputed leader of the global order is in a state of terminal decline. As the world moves towards a more fragmented system, the United States faces the consequences of an economic and diplomatic divorce that will significantly reshape its future prosperity and influence.

If the United States is to remain a world leader, what does this country need to do to improve international relations? What can you do to influence the US to become a more cooperative member of the world?

Pop Quiz - "The world is divorcing the US."

#	Question	Yes	No
1	Are you aware that the world is moving away from the Petrodollar and the use of the SWIFT monetary system?		
2	Are you aware that the value of the US dollar is declining due to the rise of alternative reserve currencies?		
3	Are you aware that the "America First Policy" has been implemented in a manner that harms our allies and trading partners?		
4	Are you aware that the US withdrawal from world organizations has significantly damaged our influence on the world stage?		
5	Are you aware that the erratic foreign trade and immigration policies implemented in 2025 and beyond, have reversed existing norms and created distrust of the US government.		

10 Strategies for a more equitable future.

Tackling Inequality in the United States:

Strategies for a More Equitable Future

Inequality in the United States has reached, and in some cases exceeded, levels not seen since the Gilded Age of the late 19th century. While the nation has seen periods of economic growth, this prosperity has been heavily concentrated at the top, leaving middle- and lower-income households struggling with wage stagnation, high debt, and limited social mobility. This disparity is not merely a matter of income, but a deep-seated structural issue involving wealth concentration, racial disparities, and unequal access to education and healthcare. Addressing this crisis requires a multifaceted approach, combining tax reform, labor market strengthening, and investment in human capital.

The Landscape of Inequality

The current state of inequality in the U.S. is characterized by a widening gap in both income and wealth. While the top 0.1 percent of households gained over $39.5 million between 1989 and 2022, households in the bottom 20 percent gained less than $8,500.

An example of this inequality was the UAW strike against General Motors, when approximately 48,000 UAW members walked out on Sept. 15, 2019, lasting six weeks (40 days) until Oct. 25, 2019, primarily due to disputes over wages, temporary worker paths to permanent status, and plant closures. Under the 2019 contract, UAW factory workers, specifically at General Motors, had top pay for assemblers around $65,000 annually, with wages ranging from $17–$28 an hour for in-progression workers and $28–$33 an hour for legacy workers. Including benefits, total labor costs for union workers at the Detroit three automakers exceeded $60 an hour in that period. That means the total compensation packages for UAW factory workers, including benefits and employer expenses (i.e. FICA, FUTA, Workers

Compensation insurance, etc.) totaled $60/hrs. x 2080 hours/year = $124,800/year.

At the same time the CEO of General Motors had a compensation package that was disproportionately high. In 2019, General Motors CEO, received a total compensation package of approximately $21.6 million. This figure represented a slight decrease of about 1.1% from the previous year, though she remained the highest-paid CEO among the Detroit Three automakers.

The total compensation of $124,800/ yr (including salary and benefits) for General Motors factory workers versus $21,600,000 compensation for the CEO, shows a vast disparity. In summary, the CEO makes about 173 times the income of the average factory worker. Other C level executives within General Motors made significant compensation, being many times the factory workers compensation.

This income inequity should be narrowed, if the United States is to regain its place as the strongest country in the world. A strong middle class, with home ownership and equity in the employing company, generates a stable community, lower crime rates and more community cohesiveness. The ideas presented in this statement are generally accepted in sociology, economics, and urban studies. A more equitable financial spread should result in less poverty, lower crime rate, full employment, and a stronger sense of community. If the US is to truly regain its title of being a world leader, we need to lead the world in treating our own residents.

The rich get richer and the poorer get poorer. The formula for a declining society.
Equitable pay for all, ensuring food clothing, shelter, transportation, education, and healthcare, is the formula for a strong, emerging society.

Wealth inequality is even more extreme than income inequality, with the top 1 percent holding nearly 31 percent of total wealth in 2024. This concentration is perpetuated by investment income growing faster than wages, and a tax system that often favors capital over labor.

Furthermore, these disparities are deeply rooted in racial and gender lines. The legacy of systemic discrimination, including redlining and unequal educational opportunities, has resulted in a significant wealth gap; between 1989 and 2022, the wealth of the average White household grew 7.2 times more than the average Black household.

Structural Causes

Several factors have contributed to the rising inequality over the past four decades:

- **Declining Labor Union Power:** The decline of unions, partly due to globalization and automation, has diminished workers' bargaining power, accounting for a significant portion of rising inequality.

> **Technological Change and "Winner-Take-Most" Markets:** Information technology has increased demand for highly skilled workers while automating low-skill jobs, allowing top earners to command massive rewards.

> **Financialization:** The shift of the economy toward finance, rather than production, has led to explosive growth in executive compensation, with CEO pay rising 940% from 1978 to 2018 compared to 12% for typical workers.

> **Policy Choices:** Tax policies have become less progressive, and labor standards have not kept pace with the cost of living, widening the divide.

Tackling Economic Inequality: Tax Reform

A primary solution to rising inequality is reforming the tax code to ensure the wealthy pay their fair share.

1. **Implementing a Federal Wealth Tax:** A direct, annual tax on the net worth of the ultra-wealthy could raise significant revenue while curbing the explosive growth of fortunes at the top. For instance, a 2% tax on wealth over $5 million, 3% above $50 million, and 5% above $1 billion could raise over half a trillion dollars annually.

2. **Raising Corporate Taxes:** Increasing the corporate tax rate, which was significantly reduced by the 2017 Tax Cuts and Jobs Act, is essential for reducing income inequality.

3. **Closing Tax Loopholes:** Taxing capital gains at the same rate as wage income, and limiting deductions that disproportionately benefit high earners, would create a more equitable system.

Strengthening Labor and Wages

To ensure economic growth benefits all workers, the following actions are needed:

1. **Raising the Federal Minimum Wage:** Modernizing the minimum wage

is a crucial step to providing an income floor and reducing poverty.

2. **Supporting Collective Bargaining:** Making it easier for workers to join unions and bargain collectively can help reverse the decline in worker leverage and improve wage growth.

3. **Expanding Worker Protections:** Strengthening and enforcing labor standards is necessary to protect workers in low-wage sectors.

Investing in Human Capital: Education and Health

Inequality of opportunity restricts social mobility and stifles long-term economic growth.

1. **Improving Educational Access:** High-wealth families are 29 percentage points more likely to complete two years of college than low-wealth families. Investing in early childhood education and fair funding for public schools can bridge this achievement gap.

2. **Addressing Health
    Disparities:** Because wealth is
    connected to health, targeted
    interventions are needed to reduce
    disparities in mortality and morbidity,
    particularly for marginalized
    communities.

3. **Eliminating Student Debt:** Relieving
    student debt can directly boost the
    financial security of low- and middle-
    income families, enabling greater
    economic participation.

The Role of Social Innovation

In addition to top-down policy changes,
social innovation is required to address
structural inequalities. This includes using
technology to increase access to essential
services and reducing bias in automated
systems. For example, developing "Just
Tech" approaches ensures that technology
serves marginalized communities rather than
Surveilling or discriminating against them.

Conclusion

Large corporations make more money when the general population prospers. The social benefits of having a very large and strong middle class, is reduced crime, reduced poverty, and increased healthcare. The economic benefits included, increased individual savings, better housing, better education, and an overall sense of security. All of these conditions lead to a better feeling of community.

Inequality is not an inevitable outcome of a modern economy; it is the result of specific, economic and political, choices. Tackling it requires a comprehensive, long-term commitment to reshaping the economic system.

By investing in education, strengthening labor rights, and implementing a fair tax system that taxes wealth, the United States can foster a more inclusive and sustainable economy. The cost of inaction is social unrest, slower growth, and a shrinking middle class. This cost is too high to ignore.

Pop Quiz - "Strategies for a more equitable future."

#	Question	Yes	No
1	Do you recognize the financial and social inequities in the US?		
2	Are you active in promoting any social or economic reforms?		
3	Are you actively supporting the eradication of health disparities in the US?		
4	Are you supporting tax reforms to ensure each person and corporation pays a fair and equitable tax rate?		
5	Do you actively read about and investigate local and national issues that impact your community?		

11 Corporate Leaders have a responsibility to fix the US

Many corporations in the US donated to political campaigns, via Political Action Committees (PACs) and other means. Often times those donations were made in support of politicians who supported a more conservative and therefore more restrictive view of life in the US, in other words, "the Old Guard." Often times corporate leaders look to what worked last year and kept doing the same thing. They often ignored or minimized the potential impacts of demographic changes and technology on their customer base and/or their employee base. Consider these two examples of corporate actions and their implications on the corporate bottom line.

First consider the major retail corporation who announced they would eliminate their internal Diversity, Equity, and Inclusion (DEI) program in January 2025, immediately following a similar announcement by a major political figure. Corporate leaders did not realize that while their actions seemed to be in line with a political view point, those same actions insulted their employee base, and more importantly their customer base. The customers responded in mass by shopping elsewhere. Sales plummeted nationwide. By August of the same year, the COE was removed from office. Stock prices dropped from about $132/share in January 2025 to a low of about $86/share by November of the same year. This amounted to about a 35% lose in stock value and market cap in 11 months. The corporate leaders did not realize that insulting their customers would have tangible financial consequences. The lesson learned is that corporate leaders need to listen to their customer base before making political statements.

Second, A large beverage production corporation, drives Diversity, Equity, and Inclusion (DEI) as a core business strategy, aiming for 50% women in leadership and U.S. racial/ethnic representation reflecting national census data by 2030.

Programs focus on talent development, supplier diversity, and community empowerment, such as the "5by20" initiative for women, while fostering an accessible, inclusive workplace. Their customer base is aware of this DEI strategy and supports it by continuously buying the company's products.

Product sales, market cap, and stock prices have remained high. That corporation showed a 25% increase in stock value in calendar year 2025. Their customer base responded to their corporate core values very favorably.

Publicly supporting Diversity, Equity, and Inclusion (DEI) programs helps corporations drive higher financial performance, boost innovation, and improve employee retention. These initiatives cultivate a positive, inclusive culture that enhances brand reputation, attracts top talent—particularly among Millennials and Gen Z—and fosters a sense of belonging, which increases employee engagement by up to 83%. By appealing to Millennials, Gen Z, Gen Alpha and Gen Beta, corporations remain in touch with their current and future customers.

Large and small corporations also have a responsibility to help build a country that reflects the core values of its population. This goal can be accomplished by recognizing the changes in our work force and our customer base.

Please take a few minutes to understand how the labor force and therefore the population in the US has changed in the past few decades. The labor force has undergone a radical shift from the post-WWII "baby boom" era to a period of contraction and aging. The basis of this information comes from LinkedIn, Zip recruiters, and other employee recruiting sites.

- ➢ **Aging and Multi-generational Workforces:** In 1950, the median age was lower, and the labor force was dominated by younger workers. By 2026, the number of workers aged 65+ has surged by 117% over the last two decades. Corporations now manage up to five generations simultaneously, facing "clogged" promotion ladders as older employees work longer and delayed retirements limit upward mobility for younger talent.

- ➢ **The Gender Revolution:** Female labor force participation rose from roughly 34% in 1950 to a peak of 60% by 2000. While this growth has leveled off, modern corporations depend on women for high-skill roles, though they face a shrinking pool of women for "hands-on" service and care roles. However, this situation has created an opening for people to fill jobs, that were previously considered non-traditional roles for men or women.

- ➢ **Labor Scarcity:** As birth rates remain below replacement levels, the U.S.-born labor force is projected to shrink annually through the next decade. This creates a "talent war" where employers must raise wages and offer flexible benefits to attract candidates from a slowly growing pool.

- ➢ **Immigration as a Lifeline:** By 2026, immigration has become the primary driver of population growth. According to the U.S. Bureau of Labor Statistics (BLS), a more diverse labor force is essential for sustained economic productivity. If corporate sales are to increase, products, services, and employment must appeal to immigrants.

2. Evolution of the Customer Population

Customer segments have fragmented, moving away from the mass-market norms of the 1950s toward highly personalized and culturally diverse niches.

- ➢ **The Rise of the "Silver Economy":** With the first Baby

Boomers turning 80 in 2026, wealth is concentrated in older cohorts. Corporations are redesigning retail spaces with wider aisles and "click and collect" services to accommodate an aging clientele that prioritizes convenience and quality.

- ➢ **Unprecedented Diversity:** Unlike the 1950s, the modern consumer base is increasingly multi-ethnic. Projections from the U.S. Census Bureau indicate that by 2045, no single racial or ethnic group will hold a majority. Brands like Coca-Cola have survived by shifting from 1950s-style mass marketing to influencer-led, culturally nuanced campaigns.

- ➢ **Digital and Social Shifts:** There is a sharp generational divide in purchasing behavior. 75% of Boomers still prefer traditional research reports, which proved useful prior to the 2000s. Millennials make buying decisions by heavily researching products online, prioritizing peer reviews, social proof, and brand authenticity over traditional marketing. They are price-conscious, frequently using mobile apps for discounts, and value convenience, such as fast shipping and seamless, omnichannel experiences. An estimated 78% of Gen Z makes buying decisions through a research-heavy, social-first approach, relying on peer reviews, influencer recommendations, and brand alignment with ethical values. They prioritize authenticity, sustainability, and transparency, frequently using platforms like TikTok and Instagram for discovery. They often combine online research with in-person shopping, using digital channels for convenience while valuing physical experiences.

➤ **Geographic Redistribution:** The post-1950s suburban explosion continues to shape retail, with a modern shift toward "surban" environments—affordable, urban-like suburbs where consumers increasingly choose renting over owning.

Corporate Implications

To remain competitive, corporations must pivot from efficiency-based models to flexibility-based ones. This includes adopting Inclusive Leadership to manage diverse teams and utilizing Advanced Data Analytics to predict the shifting needs of a heterogeneous customer base.

In 2026 and beyond, recruitment is shifting from a volume-driven process to a precision-led strategy, necessitated by a shrinking U.S.-born labor pool. To maintain growth despite these structural labor supply constraints, corporations are adopting the following five strategies:

1. Shift to "Skills-First" Hiring
As traditional degree pathways fail to keep pace with rapid technological shifts (like AI adoption), 27.3% of U.S. employers have already removed degree requirements from their job postings
.

> Recruitment Focus: Prioritizing demonstrated abilities and role-specific certifications over educational pedigree.
> Assessment Tools: Increased use of skills-based assessments, portfolio reviews, and project-based evaluations to identify talent in diverse, non-traditional pools.

2. Managing the Multi-Generational Workforce

By 2026, recruiters are navigating a unique paradox: Gen Z and Millennials make up 74% of the workforce, yet the number of workers aged 65+ has grown by 117% over the last two decades.

- ➢ Gen Z Attraction: Recruitment marketing emphasizes mental health benefits, work flexibility, and social impact.
- ➢ Senior Retention: Forward-thinking firms are redesigning roles for "aging in place," offering flexible hours for older workers to preserve institutional knowledge and mitigate the loss of judgment from mass retirements.

3. AI as a Co-Recruiter

AI has moved from an experimental tool to an operational baseline.

- ➢ Automation: AI agents now handle roughly 80% of transactional activities, including initial screening, candidate Q&A, and interview scheduling.
- ➢ Human Differentiation: As AI manages volume, human recruiters are specializing in relationship building and persuading passive candidates who are less likely to respond to automated outreach.

4. Radical Transparency and Stability

In a "low-hire, low-fire" environment where 73% of workers plan to stay in their current roles ("job hugging"), attracting talent requires radical transparency.

➤ Pay Transparency: With mandates expanding across states like NY, CA, and WA, salary disclosure is now a core requirement for a credible employer brand.

➤ Stability Signals: Candidates are increasingly vetting employers for financial health and leadership quality before applying.

5. Building "Internal Talent Pipelines"

Because external labor supply is constrained by declining birth rates and restricted immigration, corporations are pivoting to recruiting from within.

➤ Strategy: Investing in upskilling and reskilling existing employees to fill specialized gaps, particularly in AI governance, green energy, and healthcare.

➤ Retention as Recruitment: Succession planning has become a top priority to prevent critical skill gaps when older professionals retire.

In summary, corporate growth in 2026 and beyond will require a DEI approach to customers, suppliers, and employees.

Pop Quiz - "Corporate leaders have a responsibility to fixing the US."

#	Question	Yes	No
1	Are you willing to grow your corporation while implementing corrections to the disparities in today's US??		
2	Do you want new customers, which includes the changing demographics in this country?		
3	Will you welcome new employees regardless of race, age, sex, or citizen?		
4	Are you open to fair and equitable contracts with a diverse pool of suppliers?		
5	Are you willing to accommodate employee needs from multiple generations?		

12 Only US citizens can repair and save the USA.

Saving the USA requires active citizen engagement to strengthen democratic institutions, foster national unity, and address systemic issues. Individual citizens, elected officials, and corporate leaders each have a role in repairing our nation.

Key actions include protecting voting rights, engaging in local community service, developing a responsible, in-depth information diet, and holding officials accountable to restore civil discourse.

The first thing citizens need to do is to open their eyes and educate themselves on what is happening within the leadership in the USA. We need to educate ourselves on the impacts on our actions or lack of actions in participating in the management of life in the USA. We have the power of the internet in our hands daily. When you have a question about our laws, customs, and lawful administration thereof, "Google it!"

Seek the truth, not the inflammatory soundbites on TV, Streaming, and radio shows. Be informed. And remember Freedom isn't free!

I. Strengthening Democratic Institutions
The foundation of the United States rests on the participation of its citizens. Equal rights for all, has to continue to be a foundational belief and principle of our country. Protecting this foundation involves:

➢ **Defending Voting Rights:** Ensuring that all eligible voters have a voice requires passing federal and state-level laws that eliminate discriminatory barriers and increase fair representation, such as moving toward electoral systems that encourage consensus-driven, rather than polarized, politics.

➢ **Engaging at the Local Level:** Democracy is strongest at the grassroots level. Citizens can actively engage in local government meetings, serve on boards, and participate in community service to address local issues before they become national crises.

> **<u>Enhancing Civic Education</u>:** An informed citizenry is essential. Understanding the Constitution, specifically the 14th Amendment's protection of due process and equal protection, is necessary for recognizing and combating systemic injustices.

> **<u>Holding each elected official accountable</u>**: Each citizen should remain engaged in communicating and evaluating the performance of each of our elected officials. For instance, you should let each congressman know whether you prove of their actions in Washington DC.

> **II. Fostering National Unity and Discourse**
Overcoming political polarization is crucial for the nation's stability. Elected officials must lead this effort, with the encouragement, support, and participation of the general population.

- ➤ **<u>Cultivating a Healthy Information Diet</u>:** To combat the effects of authoritarianism and misinformation, citizens must move away from "doomscrolling" on social media and cable networks. Replacing sensationalized news with in-depth, accurate, and diverse information sources enables better decision-making.

- ➤ **<u>Restoring Civil Discourse</u>:** Citizens must look beyond sound bites and challenge politicians who avoid complex debates. Promoting respectful dialogue across political lines helps build a broader, pro-democracy movement.

- ➤ **<u>Fostering Patriotism and Service</u>:** Echoing historical calls to action, such as JFK's "ask not what your country can do for you," citizens can save the nation by serving in their communities, volunteering, and mentoring, rather than waiting for top-down solutions.

> ### III. Addressing Systemic Economic and Social Challenges

> **Tackling Inequality:** Rebuilding the middle class is necessary for economic stability. This involves advocating for policies that bridge the widening income gap and ensure a robust safety net for those in need.

> **Promoting Social Cohesion:** Actively working against divisive rhetoric and embracing diversity strengthens the social fabric. Ensuring equal protection under the law for all citizens, as promised by the 14th Amendment, is crucial for internal peace.

> ### IV. Ensuring National Security and Stability
> **Supporting Resilient Infrastructure:** Citizens can push for investments that make the nation's infrastructure, from energy grids to cybersecurity, resistant to foreign threats and natural disasters.

<u>**Holding Leadership**</u>

<u>**Accountable:**</u> Citizens must demand that elected officials prioritize the nation's long-term health over short-term political gains. This involves using formal mechanisms—voting, lobbying, and contacting representatives—to ensure government accountability.

"Freedom is <u>NOT</u> free!"

V. Corporate Leadership Accountability: Corporations should build respect and equity with employees, customers, suppliers, and international partners. Corporate leaders and managers should be aware of the changing demographics of the US since 1950 and the projected changes for the future. The "Browning of America", Chapter 3 discusses the changes in US demographics.

The shift in U.S. demographics from 1950 to 2026 represents a transition from a rapidly growing, youthful, and relatively homogeneous population to one that is older, more diverse, and growing at its slowest rate in decades. For corporations, this evolution fundamentally alters both the supply of talent and the nature of consumer demand.

Corporations should recognize that their employee base and their customer base have changed dramatically since the 1950's. A more inclusive thought process in these areas will lead to better sales results. More inclusive thinking in the boardroom, would generate more relevant products and services which will be appealing and useful to your ever evolving customer base.

In summary, saving the USA is not the job of one leader or one party, but a continuous, collective effort by its citizens. By focusing on strengthening democracy, fostering unity, tackling economic inequality, and ensuring security, Americans can ensure the nation's longevity. This requires moving from passive observation to active participation in the daily maintenance of this great country. Get involved. Participate in political organization, town halls, grass roots initiatives, and more. Here are a few things you can do to be more politically active.

- ➢ **Electoral Participation:** Vote in all local, state, and national elections, assist with voter registration drives, or work directly on political campaigns.

- ➢ **Direct Advocacy:** Contact representatives via phone, email, or in-person meetings to support or oppose legislation. Sign petitions and participate in public protests or rallies to draw attention to issues.

- ➢ **Community & Local Engagement:** Join local political parties, clubs, or non-partisan organizations. Attend city council meetings, school board meetings, or join community boards to influence local policy.

- ➢ **Political Education & Communication:** Stay informed by reading diverse news sources and discussing issues with others. Use social media to share information and advocate for causes.

➢ **Support Organizations:** Donate time, money, or expertise to nonprofit advocacy groups, charities, or grassroots movements.

Taking these steps helps citizens shape policies, hold officials accountable, and foster community, with opportunities to get involved at local, state, and federal levels.

Pop Quiz - "Only US citizens can repair and save the USA."

#	Question	Yes	No
1	Are you active in any grass roots political organizations?		
2	Will you study political issues in dept, as opposed to believing the headlines and sound bites?		
3	Will you track inequities within your city, county, state, and nation?		
4	Will you hold your elected officials accountable for their actions, good or bad?		
5	Will you commit time, energy, and other resources to build win-win scenarios for your fellow constituents?		

13 Conclusion

Take a moment to review your answers from each chapter quiz. Then think about them and discuss them with family and friends. Then discuss them with strangers at work and community events. Can you understand the viewpoint of others? Has this book assisted you in understanding your own opinions and viewpoints?

Who are you in 2026 test results. Score yourself.			
Chap #	Moral test results. Add up your answers by chapter	Yes	No
1	Introduction		
2	Chaos Years		
3	The Pledge of Allegiance		
4	The Browning of America		
5	Love Thy Neighbor as Thyself		
6	Do you believe in the Caste System?		
7	Moral Crisis of the US Immigration System		
8	Do you want "Win – Win" or "Win – Lose" Scenarios?		
9	The world is divorcing the US		
10	Strategies for a more equitable future		
11	Corporate leaders have a responsibility to fixing the US		
12	Only US citizens can repair and save the USA		
Totals			

We, the citizens of the United States, can be better than we were a few years ago, and certainly better than our ancestors. We can build an inclusive society. We do not need to repeat the sins of our ancestors? We know how to live in a moral environment. We just have to treat each other in a fair and equitable manner. Each and every person in the US has a moral obligation to influence the moral standards and behaviors in this country. We can make life in the US very good for all, or a nightmare for some.

We should recognize the lessons learned from the NAZI regime of 1933 to 1945. We do not need to repeat these mistakes in any form or fashion. However, it looks like we are headed there now.

The next block of data is from the Holocaust Encyclopedia. I added a column to illustrate similarities between the groups that the NAZI regime targeted and the groups the US government is targeting now. People have died in the US for standing up for their rights. Why are we repeating the sins of earlier generations of humans?

Do you want the US to be a world leader or world bully/persecutor/ dominator?

Will you stand by and take action to ensure we live up to the foundational principles of our Constitution and the "Pledge of Allegiance"?

Corporations, organizations, and individuals must work together to ensure the United States becomes a world leader again.

Groups persecuted by NAZI Germany	# Deaths	Groups persecuted in the US today
Jews	6,000,000	Religious persecution
Soviet Prisoners of War	3,3000,000	Combatants
Soviet citizens	7,000,000	Immigrants
Romani People	200,000 – 500,000	Immigrants
Polish People	3,000,000	Immigrants
People with Disabilities	300,000	Disenfranchised
Jehovah's Witnesses	200,000+	Religious persecution
Serbian		Immigrants
Homosexuals	100,000+	LBGTQ+
Afro Germans	100,000+	African Americans
Dissidents (anyone who disagreed with Hitler)	100,000+	News casters, talk show hosts, politicians, etc.

Lesson learned – Dictatorships eventually turn on everyone, even the privileged.

<u>What</u> are <u>you</u> going to do to improve this country?

When?

Where?

How? &

How Often?